Recuerda

Burgos

Silos and Covarrubias

Text: Enrique del Rivero

Translation: EURO:TEXT (Martin Gell)

Photographs: Justino Díez
Enrique del Rivero (pages 15, 58-59, 71, 78, 79 y 80b),
Oronoz (pages 21, 52 y 55), Francisco Díez (pages 31c y 80a), Foto Santi (pages 49, 50 y 51),
Imagen M.A.S. (pages 64a y 64b) and Ángel Alonso (pages 18, 72-73, 74, 75, 76, 77a y 77b).

Lay-out: Gerardo Rodera

Cover design: Alfredo Anievas

© EDITORIAL EVEREST, S. A.
Carretera León-La Coruña, km 5 - LEÓN
ISBN: 84-241-3771-X
Legal deposit: LE. 825-1995
Printed in Spain

EDITORIAL EVERGRÁFICAS, S. L.
Carretera León-La Coruña, km 5
LEÓN (Spain)

Recuerda

Burgos

Silos

and Covarrubias

INDEX

THE ORIGINS

The town of Burgos is located right at the heart of the varied landscapes and ecosystems that make up the present-day province of the same name. Geomorphologically speaking, Burgos lies on the plains of the great sedimentary basin of the Duero, its urban framework resting on materials belonging to the Miocene basement and the Quaternary fluvial environment. Protected by a long succession of hills - on which the original defensive bulwark was established - over the centuries the town has sprawled down those steep hillsides in search of the flat, extensive fertile plain formed at the middle of their courses by the Rivers Arlanzón and Vena.

Historical Memory of a Town

Looking out from the highest point of the restored *Parque del Castillo,* the traveller can let his imagination run free and be swept away on a swift journey through the history of the town. To be found at the archaeological sites of the Castle itself are the remains of the first stable settlement in Burgos, which, dated as being 4,000 years old, belongs to the Campanulate Civilization. It is almost certain that subsequent to the fall of the Roman Empire, during the Visigothic era and even at the time of the Moslem invasion - some Arab chroniclers refer to the devastation of *Burdgia* by an Islamic military expedition in 863 -, a series of small, exclusively agrarian settlements existed within the area defined by the hills of Burgos, forming the embryo of the Christian defensive bastion which would give rise to the town of Burgos. The 9th century was largely marked by a succession of battles waged between the Christians from the north and the Moslems for control over the countryside and mountains of the central and southern Burgos area. The great zeal of the former in re-populating conquered areas, under the careful command of the Asturian monarchs, led to the foundation and fortification of a series of towns in order to guarantee military control of roads and border crossings. Such was the genesis of Burgos.

A view of Burgos from the castle vantage point.

The town's origins lie in its medieval castle.

Equestrian statue of Count Diego Porcelos.

A Place in History

According to the records of the *Anales Castellanos Primeros,* the *Anales Compostelanos* and the *Cronicón Burgense,* the town and castle of Burgos were founded in 884 by Count Diego Rodríguez Porcelos on the orders of the Asturian king, Alfonso III. Very soon the embryo arose of what centuries later would become a robust fortress and an important walled city.

The first urban layout of Burgos was clearly of a military and defensive nature, comprising a fortress at the top of the hill and the original wall protecting the hamlet that spread down the hill's sheltered southern side. Rapidly the number of peoples coming to the newly-built fortress in search of protection from the frequent Moslem raids grew - Goths, Basques, Cantabrians, Jews and Mozarabs. Within the walled enclosure streets were laid out, hugging the contours of the land and forming early neighbourhoods that arose around several primitive churches such as *Santa María la Blanca, San Andrés, Santa Coloma* and *Viejarrúa.*

An image of modern-day Burgos.

Count Diego Porcelos commands the town from the Arch of Santa María.

Owing to its strategic and privileged geographical location, Burgos quickly became a true crossroads at which the main medieval paths and roads across the Castilian meseta converged, namely the road connecting the centre of the Peninsula with the Biscay ports, and the vital east-west axis that followed the ancient *Via Aquitana* and which in time would become the influential Pilgrims' Route to Santiago. This role as a 'crossroads' was to prove crucial for the town's future economic development, which was based on its commercial activity.

As early as the 11th century the original urban area of Burgos, which had evolved on either side of a long street - the present-day *Calle Fernán González* -, could no longer cope with the rise in population affecting the town. Due to the fact that it was the capital of a great kingdom bordered to the south by the River Tagus and had become an important episcopal see - the latter was transferred here from Oca in 1075 - and above all owing to the influence of the main Pilgrims' Route to Santiago, a gateway for the cultural and artistic trends of Europe, Burgos was to reflect a spectacular demographic, social and economic growth.

The Arch of San Esteban still retains its Mudéjar flavour.

A Disputed Fortress

The scanty ruins that form the remains of the fortress fail to do justice to the great historical and artistic value acquired by the latter over the centuries. The various occasions on which the Castle of Burgos was besieged or destroyed in the course of its long history are too many to mention. Alfonso VII seized it from the Aragonese, Henry II laid siege to it against the tenacious resistance of the Jews, the Catholic Kings were at the centre of the most important of the sieges, aimed at producing the surrender of Juana *la Beltraneja,* the *Comuneros* drew strength from the castle in their fight against royal authority, and finally it was besieged by the allied troops under the Duke of Wellington. This siege failed, but a few months later on 13th June 1813, the French forces fled from Burgos, blowing up the castle on their retreat. Other uses to which the fortress was put were those of a prison - during the reigns of Alfonso X and Peter I the Cruel - and a regal palace. Henry III was the monarch who converted it into a luxury residence featuring elegant rooms in *Mudéjar* style. Before leaving the parade ground, one can explore the mysterious and legendary underground structures of the *Cueva del Moro* and the *Pozo Central.*

The Vantage-Point and the Castle Park

On leaving the main enclosure of the fortress, it is a must to visit the remains of the Church of *Santa María la Blanca,* situated on the esplanade next to the Obelisk fountain. Recent archaeological excavations have confirmed the importance of this primitive place of worship in Burgos, which was built in early Romanesque style over more ancient remains. On the way down to the town, one can stop awhile at the refurbished Castle mirador. From this most privileged vantage point, apart from getting one's strength back at the modern and well-run restaurant and coffee-shop, one can admire the view over the entire urban extension of Burgos. Convenient stone steps lead the visitor down, under the protection of a conifer wood that covers an area that once held the most important districts of the town, to the proximity of the wall and the *San Esteban Gate.* The latter is a good example of 14th-century Mudéjar art.

Detail of the Arch of Fernán González.

Monument commemorating the site of El Cid's house.

Three Castilian heroes

If one is searching for the medieval past of these high areas of the town, the best thing is to follow the course of *Calle Fernán González*. In this old street, formerly known as *Cal Tenebregosa*, three commemorative monuments have been erected over the centuries in honour of the most renowned heroes of Burgos. The first to be encountered on our way, and also the oldest, is the triumphal arch of Fernán González, dating from 1586. Master Juan Ortega de Castañeda was commissioned by the town council with the construction of this monument, which features a wide semicircular arch flanked by columns and crowned by several coats of arms. Rising up a little further on is the funeral monument which, topped by a large obelisk, honours the nineteenth-century guerrilla Juan Martín *el Empecinado*. It was built in 1844 by Agustín de Marcoastu. The last such landmark is the so-called *Solar del Cid*, a modest monument erected at the site on which according to tradition once stood the house of Rodrigo Díaz de Vivar. It was built in 1784 following the designs of José Cortés.

Before leaving the walled enclosure, the traveller should bear in mind that the last steps he takes here lead him through the former Jewish quarter of Burgos, which in Castile was second in importance only to that of Toledo. Burgos was to thank its Jewish community for many of its doctors, writers and philosophers, and some Jews even came to figure amongst the most faithful advisers to the Castilian monarchs. In the early 15th century, in what is one of the most fascinating twists in the town's history, a local rabbi, Pablo de Santa María, became archbishop of Burgos.

Paseo de los Cubos

A nice way to return to the town centre is to follow the route skirting the old medieval walls, along the pleasant, well laid out *Paseo de los Cubos*. The sections of wall lining this avenue constitute the best preserved remains of the walled enclosure that as from the 13th century, the times of King Alfonso X the Wise, completely encircled the town. Standing very high and built using good masonry, the enclosure features alternating crenellated curtain walls and semicircular reinforcement towers.

The legendary figure of El Cid Campeador stands out against the clear skies of Burgos.

*The Church of San Esteban and the old town,
from the castle vantage.*

A JEWEL FOR MANKIND

In 1984, exactly 1,100 years after Count Diego Rodríguez Porcelos had founded the castle and town of Burgos, UNESCO declared Burgos Cathedral as belonging to the Heritage of Mankind. Although the two dates coincided purely by chance, this fact serves to further highlight the great importance for Burgos of the town's primary monumental construction.

As a result of the said declaration we have all become heirs and therefore guardians of the cathedral, that enormous enterprise which involved the participation of dozens of bishops and architects, hundreds of sculptors and thousands of carvers from many different countries. The latter have given rise to a magnificent architectural monument that fascinates all who come to admire it and which has a highly communicative nature, a reflection of the genius and spirit of all those responsible.

The greatness of a piece of monumental architecture is not only determined by the collection of works of art that make up its structure and content - one must also take into account the way it is spatially integrated into its environment. Such is the case of Burgos Cathedral, a building whose aesthetic value is considerably enhanced by the contrast established between its matchless architectural volume and the urban forms that lie at its feet. Walking around the outside is a good way to take in the whole artistic and spiritual message embraced by the stones of Burgos Cathedral.

The cathedral sanctuary seen from Calle Fernán González.

*◀ Royal façade
of the cathedral
seen from Plaza
Santa María.*

*Unusual view
of the cathedral
dome and transept.*

Plaza de Santa María

The best place to start off from is the square that opens out at the feet of the cathedral's impressive main façade. Indeed, from the *Plaza de Santa María*, one can contemplate one of the best-known and most characteristic views of Burgos Cathedral. The basic layout of this western front, the inspiration for which is to be found in the cathedrals of Paris and Rheims, is one of three levels crowned by two square side towers and was designed under the auspices of the founder bishop of the cathedral, Mauricio. Construction having been concluded in the second half of the 13th century, less than two-hundred years were to pass before another illustrious local prelate, Alonso de Cartagena, entrusted the German master Juan de Colonia with the erection of the daring spires that top the twin towers.

At the beginning of the narrow *Calle de Santa Agueda* we come to *Calle de Nuño Rasura*. Formerly referred to as *Calle de la Canongía,* a great number of canons and priests that served at the nearby cathedral once lived in this street. From this calm pedestrianized street one can enjoy a good example of the contrast between the great stone volumes of the cathedral and the modest houses stretching out beneath it.

Detail of the fountain in Plaza Santa María.

transept and reveals the structure of its single vessel. Its three levels, namely its doorway - constituting one of the masterpieces of Spanish Gothic sculpture -, its great rose window and its ornamentation of openwork arches, are accompanied by large buttresses and pinnacles which add weight to the visual impact of the whole.

Before continuing on our tour of the cathedral perimeter, we must stop to admire the strange drain that appears right at the corner of the cloister and which for many centuries served as a prison for priests. *Calle de la Paloma* runs parallel to one of the passages of the lower cloister of the cathedral. Pedestrians have the privilege of being able to walk through the said cloister and out into *Calle de Diego Porcelos.* By means of this old street called *Malburguete,* the visitor can reach *Las Llanas* and consequently come across the cathedral sanctuary.

Visitors facing the Sarmental doorway.

Plaza del Sarmental

Also located within the former Santa María district is the present-day *Plaza del Rey San Fernando.* From this privileged point in the town it is easy to perceive the difference in level between the cathedral's southern façade and that which gives onto the current *Calle de Fernán González.* Many of the constructional elements of the cathedral have been conditioned by this slope. Here, the visitor can take in the entire *Sarmental* façade and doorway, the towers crowned by spires, the lantern of the *Capilla de la Presentación* and the uppermost section of the *cimborrio* or dome.

One of the most surprising facts about the construction of the cathedral is the speed with which the initial work was carried out. Thus, barely eight years passed between the ceremony marking the laying of the first stone - held on 20th July 1221 and presided over by Bishop Mauricio and King Fernando III - and the celebration of the first mass by the very same local prelate. The *Sarmental* façade, concluded in around 1240, stands at the southern end of the

The Gospel aisle.

The Constables' Chapel

The unmistakeable silhouette of the *Capilla de los Condestables* and the *Pellejería* doorway are the two characteristic features of the building that are revealed to us before we make our way up well laid out steps to *Calle Fernán González.* Our tour of the cathedral exterior has allowed us to perceive the full extent of the difference in level between the lower and upper parts of the building. Indeed, the 13th-century doorway that opens out from the northern façade is known not only under the names of La Coronería and *Los Apóstoles,* but also under that of *Puerta Alta,* or High Door. *Calle Fernán González,* which at this point was once called *Calle de la Coronería,* lead the visitor on to a flight of steps which, situated opposite the Church of San Nicolás and formerly called *Bajada del Azogue,* takes him back down to the Plaza Santa María. Still standing next to these steps are the houses in which in the late 15th century the first printing presses in Burgos were installed - editions of famous books such as *La Celestina* appeared here - and the town's first printers set up business: Fadrique Alemán de Basilea, Martín de Guía and Juan de Junta.

After touring the perimeter of the cathedral through some of the oldest streets and squares of Burgos, the traveller simply must go inside to admire the building's unique, magic interior.

The Cathedral Interior

Just after entering the cathedral - it takes a few moments for one's eyes to become accustomed to the soft, diffuse light of the interior - the visitor will be momentarily overwhelmed by the singular beauty and harmony of the forms surrounding him. It is best if one starts one's tour of the cathedral standing with one's back to the great wooden door at the main entrance, or *Puerta Real.* From this vantage point and in a single look, the observer can command all the various features of the nave. The first aspect that strikes us is its spectacular elevation which, in keeping with the classic models of French Gothic, is over twenty-five metres high. The well-designed articulation of the walls, the pointed arches resting on pillars, the triforium and the large openings divided by mullions manage to banish any sensation of compactness or heaviness.

The "Papamoscas".

*The heart of the cathedral
beats under its dome.* ▶

The *Papamoscas* Clock

Turning our eyes upwards we can see the elegant roofing structure - basically comprising ribbed vaulting - with which the nave of the cathedral was equipped, once more in a French style, in the 13th century. Before continuing our tour of the northern nave, we should take a look at one of the strangest and most emblematic features of the cathedral, namely the *Papamoscas*. The outstanding elements of the mechanism of this popular clock are two articulated figures, Papamoscas and Martinillo, who have been telling the time to the citizens of Burgos for over 600 years.

Almost all the chapels that came to line the model Latin cross ground plan of the cathedral have over the centuries undergone changes regarding both their dedication and architectural structure. Such is the case of the baroque *Capilla de Santa Tecla* - the last one to be constructed - and of the adjacent *Capilla de Santa Ana*. The latter, which like nearly all the chapels in the cathedral has a markedly funerary nature, was built to perpetuate the memory of the cathedral's benefactor, Luis de Acuña. It was erected in 1477 by Juan de Colonia, at that time the best artist living in Burgos, and the chapel interior features two masterpieces by artists from the same family, namely the Gothic main altarpiece by Gil de Siloe and the Renaissance sepulchre for bishop Acuña sculpted by his son, Diego de Siloe.

The Golden Staircase and the Dome

This young and innovative architect also designed the ingenious *Escalera Dorada* presiding the northern arm of the transept. The 39 steps that make up this magnificent Renaissance staircase overcame the difference of level between the base of the cathedral and the *Puerta de la Coronería.*

It is no exaggeration to say that the heart of Burgos Cathedral beats up in its dome. After passing through a heavy bronze grille and taking up the exact position - right on top of the simple slab guarding the remains of El Cid - at the point where the two arms forming the Latin cross ground plan of the cathedral intersect, one need only look upwards in order to marvel at one of the most outstanding wonders of the cathedral: the incredible stellar vaulting that crowns the interior of the crossing lantern. Four enormous squinches support this spectacular structure which was rebuilt from 1539 to 1568 by Juan de Vallejo subsequent to the collapse of the previous Gothic lantern erected by Juan de Colonia. Before leaving the grilled interior of the *Capilla Mayor,* one should stop to admire its great Romanesque altarpiece and the beautiful choir stalls.

Diego de Siloe's "Golden Staircase".

The openwork vaulting of the Capilla de los Condestables represents the height of technical perfection in all the cathedral. ▶

A Cathedral within the Cathedral

On reaching the ambulatory after having covered the whole length - 84 metres - of the Latin cross ground plan of the cathedral, we find ourselves at the entrance to the *Capilla de los Condestables,* a veritable cathedral within the Cathedral. A splendid entrance arch protected by the most beautiful grille of the whole building - wrought by Cristóbal de Andino in 1523 - leads us into the *Capilla de la Purificación* or the Constables' Chapel. The powerful and influential personalities Pedro Fernández de Velasco and his wife Doña Mencia de Mendoza entrusted the great artist Simón de Colonia with the construction of a monumental funerary pantheon. Of large proportions, this pantheon was erected from 1482 to 1494 in a style combining the last elements of Gothic and the first manifestations of Renaissance art and represents the architectural culmination of Burgos Cathedral.

The main altarpiece of the chapel, a piece of work paradigmatic of Spanish Renaissance sculpture, was jointly crafted by Felipe de Vigarny and Diego de Siloe and is complemented by two smaller works: the Gothic *Santa Ana* altarpiece and that of *San Pedro,* likewise Renaissance.

Right at the centre of the chapel lies the sepulchre of the Constables. Attributed to Felipe de Vigarny and worked from Carrara marble, this is one of the highlights of Spanish funerary sculpture. Looking up from within the chapel, the visitor will be amazed at Simón de Colonia's beautiful and technically audacious vaulting and in particular his central openwork star, which crowns the octagonal lantern over the *Capilla de los Condestables.*

Detail of the sepulchre of Alonso de Cartagena.

The Cathedral Cloister, Museum and Collection of Relics

Surprised and taken aback by such beauty, the visitor is once again obliged to come to a halt in order to admire yet another wondrous work of art. On this occasion, it is the reliefs sculpted by Felipe de Vigarny that stand in the retro-choir of the *Capilla Mayor* or Main Chapel. The most outstanding relief is the panel which, dating from 1498, portrays the Stations of the Cross.

After the *Capilla de Santiago* and the main sacristy, we come to the cloister. Owing to the difference in level, the cathedral cloister comprises two superimposed storeys. It features a rectangular ground plan and its construction - dating from the late 13th century - is partly attributable to the master Johan Pérez. Through its large openings one can see a series of group sculptures and numerous sepulchres that have accumulated over the centuries. Its eastern section opens out - the only side that can do so due to its position - into the chapels of *El Corpus Christi, San Juan Bautista* and *Santa Catalina* which lead on through interesting façades to the cathedral Museum and Collection of Relics. Here it is best to follow the instructions of the cathedral guides.

The Christ of Burgos

Leaving behind the *Capilla de San Enrique,* we come to the transept on the Sarmental doorway side of the cathedral. From a point near this doorway one of the best views of the cathedral interior is to be gained. Just opposite the remarkable doorway leading to the cloister is the entrance to the Capilla de la Visitación. Buried in this chapel, in a beautiful late Gothic sepulchre, is Bishop Alonso de Cartagena. Further on down the Epistle aisle is the *Capilla de la Presentación.* Designed from 1519 to 1524 by Juan de Matienzo, it houses the sepulchre - fashioned by Felipe de Vigarny - of the canon Gonzalo de Lerma. On carefully closing the grille wrought by Cristóbal de Andino and before leaving the church, the visitor must, whether he be a believer or not, meditate awhile before the pathetic, sorrowful 14th-century image of the Holy Christ of Burgos, thus repeating the gesture made by the millions of pilgrims who, on their way to Santiago, have passed through this town on the Arlanzón.

After the cathedral, San Gil is the most interesting Gothic church in Burgos.

THE GOTHIC HEART OF BURGOS

There is only one thing that can be said against Burgos Cathedral, namely that its splendour overshadows the large number of Gothic churches situated in its proximity. The churches of *San Gil, San Esteban, San Nicolás* and *Santa Agueda,* which can be reached along some of the oldest streets of the town, constitute the true Gothic heart of Burgos.

Las Llanas

The protective shadow of the cathedral marks the start of our walk in search of the town's most interesting streets and churches. Lying at the feet of the sanctuary is an uneven area that throughout time has been known as *Las Llanas.* For many centuries this typical square played host to the Burgos cereal market. Such products could not be sold at any other point within the walls and moreover this was the only market that did not come directly under the jurisdiction of the council and instead belonged to the Monastery of *Las Huelgas.* The Llana de Afuera was also the site of the *Real Consulado del Mar y Casa de Contratación y Comercio.* As from the late 15th and for most of the 16th century, this institution controlled the trade, transport, insurance and financing of a large share of the goods - in particular wool - that circulated around Europe.

The Church of San Gil

By crossing the much-frequented *Plaza de la Flora,* we quickly reach the San Gil district. Rising up at the highest part of the latter and surrounded by the town walls is the church of the same name. Its original Romanesque structure was replaced in the late 13th and early 14th centuries, only to be altered once more in around 1399 on the initiative of Pedro de Camargo y García de Burgos and Bishop Juan de Villacreces. The 15th century saw the extension of the sanctuary and in the 16th two further chapels were added: the funerary *Capilla de la Natividad* and the *Capilla de la Cruz,* the latter being the work of the local architect Juan de Vallejo. San Gil is deemed to be the most beautiful and interesting of the Gothic churches in Burgos, second only to the cathedral itself. Of all the treasures that this church holds the most outstanding is the funerary Capilla de la Natividad, attributed to Juan de Matienzo. Featuring a Reinassance altarpiece and the sepulchres of its founders, this chapel is crowned by an original, completely perforated stellar vault.

The façade of San Nicolás.
Next page: The Gothic Church of San Esteban

The San Esteban District

The best way to leave the former district of leather craftsmen is to take the *Calle Hospital de los Ciegos.* As its present name would suggest, gracing this typical Burgos street in the 14th century was a hospital for the blind, the maimed and the hunchbacked. Leaving behind us the steep narrow street called *Alvar Fáñez* and with the Saldaña school - founded in the 18th century - before us, we come to *Calle de Valentín Palencia* and the area surrounding the Church of San Esteban.

Of all the districts that evolved in the shadow of the Castle, the only one to have survived the passing of time - albeit severely ravaged - is that of San Esteban. The noblest and most illustrious families in Burgos once had their ancestral homes in one of the long since vanished streets that formed a maze around the parish church. The present-day Church of San Esteban was built over a previous Romanesque construction in the last third of the 13th and the first half of the 14th centuries. Beneath a sturdy tower - whose stones

have been damaged in many of the sieges and attacks on the neighbouring castle - stands a late 13th-century façade in which one can detect the influence of the nearby cathedral. From the top of the singular choir, the work of Simón de Colonia and Nicolás de Vergara, one can admire a translucent interior divided into a nave and two aisles and which houses an interesting Diocesan Museum of the Retable.

Down to San Nicolás

From the *Plaza de Pozo Seco* - in which popular tournaments and festivities were held during the Middle Ages - the street of the same name takes us down to the district and church of San Nicolás. Generally speaking, the structure of this church belongs to the 15th century and it houses one of the artistic jewels of Burgos, namely an impressive altarpiece sculpted from stone in the early 16th century by the great artist Francisco de Colonia.

We take the present-day Calle de Fernán González and, on reaching the *Plazuela de Felipe de Abajo,* descend the steps leading steeply down to the Santa Agueda district. The long building appearing before us is the *Alhóndiga* or former Corn Exchange of Burgos. The warehouses of this great exchange - built in around 1513 - used to store wheat and barley which, particularly in times of shortage, would supply the citizens with food.

The Oath of Santa Gadea

At the entrance to the present-day Church of *Santa Agueda,* a memorial stone reminds the traveller that this was the spot where El Cid Campeador demanded that his king, Alfonso VI, should take an oath. The Romanesque church in which this legendary gesture of El Cid took place was replaced in the 15th century by the current Gothic-style church. To conclude our walk around the heart of Gothic Burgos, from the rear of *Santa Agueda* we take the narrow, winding *Calle de Embajadores* - popularly known under the exoteric and mysterious name of *Calleja de las Brujas* (Alley of the Witches) - and calmly stroll towards the cathedral, enjoying the urban surroundings on our way.

Bridge over the River Vena and the Arch of San Juan.

A TOWN ON THE PILGRIMS' ROUTE

The town of Burgos, in the proximity of which the two most important routes leading to Santiago converged - the one from Bayonne and the French Route -, constitutes one of the vital landmarks along the Spanish section of the Pilgrims' Route. For several hundred years the history and the urban development of Burgos was to be influenced by the inclusion of the town on the pilgrimage trail. Pilgrims represented the focal point of all its religious institutions, including the cathedral. Moreover, the town's 35 pilgrim *hospitals* made it the most hospitable of European cities. The following brief description of the Pilgrims' Route in Burgos aims to follow the track of the millions of pilgrims that over the centuries have tirelessly passed through Burgos on their way to the tomb of the Apostle.

The Church of La Real y Antigua at Gamonal
Our evocative journey following the trail of the Pilgrims' Route to Santiago through Burgos starts at Gamonal, today one of the town's districts. Very near to what was an once an important landmark on the pilgrims' trail - Gamonal was formerly an episcopal see - the two main medieval pilgrimage routes that passed through the province of Burgos converged. The most outstanding monumental building of Gamonal is its magnificent Church of *Nuestra Señora La Real y Antigua*. Gothic in style with certain German influences, it was built in the 14th century and preserves a high tower from the previous century. It has an aisleless nave and a Latin cross ground plan. Opposite the original Gothic portal lies a 15th-century pilgrims' stone cross whose shaft is decorated with several reliefs on the pilgrimage theme, such as an image of St James the Pilgrim.
Such was the influence exerted by the Pilgrims' Route to Santiago on the urban development of Burgos that a modern-day street map still reflects the exact historical route taken by the pilgrims. *Calle de las Calzadas,* whose origin is undeniably linked to the pilgrimage, leads us to the first landmark that greeted the pilgrims as the Pilgrims' Route wended its way through the town - namely the Monastery and Hospital of San Juan, situated in the large, well laid out square of the same name.

The Saint on the Route
The origin of this hospital complex is to be traced to the *Capilla de San Juan Evangelista* and its adjacent small hospital, founded in the second half of the 11th century under the protection of King Alfonso VI, one of the Castilian monarchs that greatly encouraged the pilgrimage. What remains of the Monastery of San Juan - which today houses the museum dedicated to the painter Marceliano Santamaría - are the ruins of its 15th-century church and the 16th-century cloister and chapterhouse. At the nearby Hospital of San Juan (nowadays the *Casa de Cultura*) which was altered in the 15th century in the times of Pope Sixtus VI, the only surviving elements are its 15th-century Gothic façade along with a number of items from its renowned apothecary.

At the end of the 11th century the reputation of the Benedictine monk Adelelmus began to spread. At the request of Alfonso VI and his wife Constanza, Adelelmus - called Lesmes in Castile - came to Spain from the Cluniac abbey of Casa Dei in France. Bearing in mind that this monk would become St Adelelmus, the king of Castile ordered the construction of a monastery at the side of the Pilgrims' Route, not far from the original Chapel of *San Juan,* and likewise dedicated it to St John the Evangelist. St *Lesmes* became the first prior of the monastery and devoted the rest of his life to the care of the most needy pilgrims.

Rising up at one of the corners of the *Plaza de San Juan* is the Church of *San Lesmes,* presided over by the equestrian sculpture of Count Diego Porcelos. Built in the late 15th century, subsequent to a succession of alterations to the original chapel, it houses the remains of the revered patron saint of Burgos. Gracing the interior of the church is an interesting collection of Gothic and Renaissance altarpieces, paintings and sepulchres.

The Church of San Lesmes.

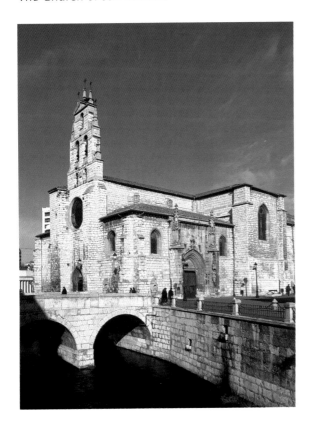

Pilgrims on their way through Burgos.

Under the Protection of the Walls

As from the last third of the 13th century - the period in which the town was encircled by strong walls - the pilgrims would pass through the said wall and over the natural fosse formed by the River Vena by means of a little bridge and the so-called *Puerta de San Juan.* One can still retrace the exact historical trail drawn by the French Route through the centre of Burgos. Along *Calle de San Juan,* the pilgrims had to cross a series of little streams which according to tradition were finally drained by St Adelelmus himself. Continuing along *Rúa de San Gil* - the present-day Calle de Avellanos -, they would come into the San Llorente district down the *Callejón del Infierno.* Leaving on its right the Church of *San Gil,* the Pilgrims' Route then ran along *Calle de Fernán González.*

There is no doubt that as from the 11th century the passing of the Pilgrims' Route through the town was to condition its urban appearance and exert a decisive influence on its social and economic evolution. Bearing witness to this is the splendour achieved by *Calle Fernán González* as a commercial axis and a residential area for the most distinguished families of Burgos.

Right: Cloister and tower of the Monastery of San Juan and Cloister interior.

Above: The Pilgrims' Route to Santiago still runs along Calle San Juan.
Down: The Pilgrims' Route to Santiago is well signposted through the Mudéjar Arch of San Juan.

In former times, pilgrims would leave Burgos through the Mudéjar Arch of San Juan.

The said street leads the visitor on to the cathedral and to one of the most unusual views of the latter. This jewel of world Gothic art undeniably exudes the atmosphere of the pilgrimage, a fact reflected by the more than thirty iconographic representations of St James the Apostle.

Leaving behind the noteworthy Church of *San Nicolás,* the Route continues through the town along *Calle Fernán González.* This street led the pilgrims out of the town, but not before they had passed a long line of shops, workshops, inns, wine-cellars, hostels and hospitals and had been caught up in the hustle and bustle of a motley local population comprising the old Christians, the Jews from the nearby *Aljama,* the Moriscos and a large number of foreigners from all parts of the world. Thus the pilgrims departed Burgos under the 14th-century Mudéjar *Arco de San Martín.*

Hospitals and Cemeteries

The Pilgrims' Route made its way down to the River Arlanzón through the San Pedro de la Fuente district and passed the *Hospital del Emperador* which, founded by Alfonso VI, was the first such institution in Burgos. Just as it did in the past, the *Puente de Malatos* - a bridge dating back as early as 1136 - today still takes pilgrims over the Arlanzón so as they may continue their journey to Santiago. On leaving the urban area and on the other side of the luxuriant park, *El Parral,* one comes across one of the most traditional landmarks of the entire Pilgrims' Route, namely the *Hospital del Rey.* Founded by Alfonso VIII in the late 12th century, its original Cistercian structure was substituted during the reign of

Emperor Charles I by a Renaissance-style building. Through the plateresque *Puerta de los Romeros* the visitor comes out into a courtyard dominated by several images of St James. The wooden doors of the church are decorated with impressive reliefs carved in the 16th century by Juan de Valmaseda and depicting a series of pilgrims. Nowadays this splendid building is home to the University of Burgos.

A stone's throw away from the hospital lies the former pilgrims' cemetery. Inside the latter there is a simple 17th-century chapel in memory of St Amaro, the French saint who after travelling to Santiago took up residence at Burgos in order to attend sick and dying pilgrims.

Pilgrims' Courtyard at the Hospital del Rey.

The Hospital del Rey *is at present home to Burgos University*

St Amaro, a famous saint in the Pilgrims' Route.

Detail of the church doorway at the Hospital del Rey.

The courtyard of the Casa de Miranda is one of the finest exponents of the Reinassance in Burgos.

SQUARES, WALKS AND GARDENS

Whereas the uneven, sloping topography of the high-lying districts of the town close to the Castle hill called for the construction of narrow, steeply rising streets with no room for squares or open spaces, when Burgos began to stretch out downwards, occupying the flatter terrain located between *Calle Fernán González* and the *Ronda de Muralla,* level streets and larger, uncluttered squares were built.

Plaza Mayor and the Town Hall

Such is the case of the original *Plaza del Mercado Menor,* which in time as to become the Main Square of Burgos. Several attempts having failed at converting the irregular perimeter of the square into a perfect rectangular shape, in the late 18th century work was begun at one end on the new Town Hall. Thus on the site of the former *Puerta de las Carretas* and following the designs of the architect Fernando González de Lara, a large Neoclassical building was erected. Constructed in Hontoria stone, it features an original façade resting on six columns and a large portico, through which one comes out into the walk called *Paseo del Espolón.* It comprises two storeys and is crowned by a balustrade and two sturdy towers on either side. The town hall was inaugurated on 17th July 1791. This harmonious square has been commanded since 1784 by a statue of Charles III, who stands aloft on a pedestal. From here, *Calle de Sombrerería* affords us the best way of continuing on our tour of the most typical streets and squares of Burgos. Featuring houses embellished by transparent, white glassed balconies, this winding street is crammed with typical *mesones* or taverns. A well-kept arcade takes us on to one of the longest arteries running through the historical centre of Burgos, namely that formed by *Calle de Paloma* and *Calle de Laín Calvo.* Turning to the right, the likewise arcaded *Calle de Paloma* is soon crossed by *Calle de Cardenal Segura.* Famous for its pharmacies, this old street leads us to the square called *Plaza de Huerto del Rey* or *Plaza de la Flora.*

The Arch of Santa María and the Cathedral make up of the best known sights in Burgos.

Plaza Mayor is still a meeting place for the citizens of Burgos

Charles III presides over the Plaza Mayor of Burgos.

The Town Hall of Burgos.

Calle Sombrerería is one of the most evocative streets in Burgos.

Plaza de la Flora

Since the mid-17th century the name given to this extensive but at the same time enclosed corner of the town is that of Flora, the Roman goddess of flowers, gardens and love. Cast in lead and gilded by Manuel Romero, a sedentary figure of the goddess presides over an original four-spouted fountain.

We can carry on our tour by going through an interesting old shop-lined passageway - dating from as early as 1848 - out into *Calle Laín Calvo*. This street follows the course of a medieval stream that was crossed by over 16 little bridges and leads off from one of the most historical squares of Burgos. On the site that since the beginning of this century has held the Neogothic palace of the *Capitanía General* (Military Headquarters), there once stood the stronghold of the Brizuelas, also known as that of the Four Towers.

View of the square called La Flora or Huerto del Rey and detail of La Flora fountain.

The Casa del Cordón is the most significant secular building in Burgos.

Baroque façade of the Church of San Lorenzo.

The Church of San Lorenzo

Just a short way down *Calle de San Juan* we find the beginning of *Calle de San Lorenzo*. This long and narrow street - also called *Cantarranas la Menor* and *Calle de los Herreros* - is where the Society of Jesus erected their school, San Salvador. 1694 witnessed the completion of the baroque Church of *San Lorenzo*, the work of the architects Bernabé de Hazas and Francisco de Pontón. It features a Greek cross ground plan and is covered at its centre by a large cupola decorated in plasterwork. Halfway down *Calle de San Lorenzo* we take another little road, San Carlos, which leads to *Cantarranas la Mayor*. Nowadays called *Calle de Almirante Bonifaz*, this was one of the most important streets in nineteenth-century Burgos and takes us on to *Calle de Santander*. At the end of the latter, known in times gone by under the lovely name of *Calle del Juego de la Pelota*, lies the square that in its day was the scene of the local Mercado Mayor, or Principal Market.

Plaza del Mercado Mayor

Since the mid-19th century this square has been divided by the houses forming the Antón arcades into the present-day *Plaza del Cordón* and *Plaza de Santo Domingo de Guzmán*. Giving out onto the former is the *Casa del Cordón,* commissioned by the Constable of Castile in the late 15th century. The main façade of this true jewel of secular architecture in Burgos is flanked by two sturdy towers that lend the building an evocative air of a palace-cum-fortress. The *Casa del Cordón* enjoyed strong links with the Discovery of America and it was here that the Catholic Kings received Christopher Columbus on his return from his second voyage to the new continent.

Monuments to El Cid

Not very far from the *Plaza de Santo Domingo de Guzmán* is the equestrian statue of El Cid Campeador. Unveiled in 1955, the bronze figure crafted by Juan Cristóbal points its sword, *Tizona,* towards the monumental San Pablo bridge which, flanked by eight stone sculptures on the theme of El Cid, has all the appearance of a triumphal way. Fashioned in the early 'fifties by the artist from Bilbao, Joaquín Lucarini, the sculptures represent the figures of Alvar Fáñez, Martín Muñoz, Martín Antolínez, Diego Rodríguez, Bishop Jerónimo, Ben Galbón, St Sisebuto and Doña Jimena.

Paseo del Espolón

Guarding the entrance to the *Paseo del Espolón* are two remarkable nineteenth-century buildings. The oldest of these is the *Teatro Principal,* the façades of which reflect an elegant conventional style designed, among others, by the architect Francisco Angoitía. The town playhouse was opened in the spring of 1858, the most relevant of its decorative elements being the modernist entrance to the Games Room and the charming *Reloj del Morito* (Clock of the Little Moor). From 1864 to 1869, in a rather more sober, classical style, the local architects Villanueva and Calleja erected the palace housing the Provincial Council. Built from Hontoria stone, it has a rectangular ground plan and features four façades embellished with classicist motifs. Inside the building is a fine selection of the town's art over the last two centuries.

One of the most welcome changes in the nearly

Detail of the Casa del Cordón.

two-hundred year existence of the *Paseo del Espolón* was the replacement of the old acacias and limes adorning its main walkway with a double line of plane trees. In the shade of their intertwined branches, the last generations of Burgos children have played and grown up. In summer, the cool microclimate of this long, shady tunnel of leaves invites people to stay awhile and chat at length on any of its benches or street cafés. The design of *El Espolón* is not completely uniform in style. The attentive observer will notice the classical traces of its original 18th-century design as an architectural garden which blend harmoniously with the more modern lines of the romantic garden of French origin.

The best place to chronologically follow the walk's evolution is at the part called *Cuatro Reyes.* In 1795, four statues from the balustrade of the Royal Palace in Madrid were erected here on the express wishes of Charles III. They portrayed personalities linked to the history of Burgos: Fernán González, Ferdinand I, Alfonso XI and Henry III. In 1868, Isabel II donated another four Neoclassical statues representing Wamba, Alfonso VI, John II and St Emilian. These were placed on pedestals at the equidistant ends of the central walkway of *El Espolón.*

Detail of one of the sculptures related to El Cid on San Pablo bridge.

Paseo del Espolón, different views. ▶

An Ecological Paradise

Constituting a live and seasonally changing part of the monumental nature of *El Espolón* is its plant life. The emblematic plane trees are joined by many other tree and shrub species, such as horse chestnuts, weeping willows, poplars, acacias, sophoras, limes, Spanish firs, American oaks, yews cut back to form elegant hedges, privets, box trees and many more, amongst which there are even some exotic, durable palms. Curiously, over the last few years there has been a promising, spontaneous recovery of plant life on the banks of the River Arlanzón. Particularly noteworthy is the section running between *El Espolón* and *El Espoloncillo,* whose aquatic and riverside vegetation provide shelter and a breeding ground for numerous species of waterfowl.

One should not leave *El Espolón* without admiring the many interesting buildings that give on to it. Standing out amidst private houses that preserve beautiful and in some cases absolutely excellent façades in the most refined of 19th-century styles is the building housing the Academy of Drawing of the *Real Consulado* of Burgos. An anchor, the symbol of the institution that arose in medieval times in order to supervise the wool trade, commands a sober pediment crafted in pure Neoclassical style.

The River Arlanzón is the geographical backbone of the town.

The bandstand on El Espolón.

Arco de Santa María

Before reaching the Arch of *Santa María,* we should take a look at the new bandstand situated on the spot once occupied by its predecessor erected in 1897. Forming the natural, urban continuation of *El Espolón* is the *Paseo de la Isla.* Uniting the two is the Arch of *Santa María.* In around 1540, the town council commissioned the Renaissance artists Juan de Vallejo and Francisco de Colonia to construct this monumental triumphal arch, in order to adorn the front of the old medieval gate of *Santa María.* Its most outstanding feature is a large retable sculpted from stone by Ochoa de Arteaga, in which a series of personalities connected with Burgos - Diego Porcelos, Laín Calvo, Nuño Rasura, Fernán González and El Cid - surround the figure of Emperor Charles I. Inside the tower one can see a large mural by the local painter Vela Zanetti dedicated to the legendary founder hero of the kingdom of Castile, Fernán González.

*Pages 41 and 42:
Different views
of the Arch of Santa
María.*

The cathedral seen from the Puente del Instituto.

At the point at which it flows through the town, the River Arlanzón has become a true ecological paradise.

Nineteenth-century Splendour

This part of Burgos has changed dramatically over the last two centuries. In the first half of the 19th century the original crenellated sections of the town walls, which stretched as far as the corner of the present-day *Calle Martínez de Campo,* were demolished and in their place a series of simple dwellings were erected which in turn were eventually replaced by elegant houses in which the most affluent families of the local 19th-century bourgeoisie resided.

In 1833 this area saw the construction of the Palace of Justice designed by the architect David Ruiz Jareño. Featuring a large rectangular ground plan and two storeys, the structure of this building is based on truly Neoclassical models. On crossing *Calle de Benito Gutiérrez,* one comes face to face with one of the most beautiful groups of buildings surviving in Burgos. The most noteworthy of all is the former *Banco de España,* in which the wise combination of red brick and Hontoria stone create a surprising decorative and functional effect.

Parque de la Isla

From the *Plaza de Castilla* onwards, the *Paseo de la Isla* becomes an extensive urban park that can accurately be described as a piece of domesticated nature. The true origins - including the etymology of its name - of the *Parque de la Isla* or Island Park are to be traced back to the Middle Ages when the local wool merchants washed and dried their produce in the proximity of the bridge called *Puente de Malatos.* The waters of the River Arlanzón and a channel from a watermill formed a small island here which, covered in poplars, was known as *Paseo de Lavadores* or Washers' Walk.

A succession of alterations and the planting of trees and shrubs have lent this walk its present-day appearance. Whilst architecturally speaking it has an interesting layout that successfully combines French symmetrical gardens with the more informal uncluttered English-style parterres, the principal attraction to be found in this park is its impressive variety of plant species. Indeed this veritable botanical garden contains some of the world's most curious trees. A whole range of exotic plant species are on display here, ranging from the giant sequoias to the equally enormous Atlas and Himalayan cedars and also including the Spanish firs and many different varieties of cypresses. Worthy of mention are the little yew groves and the numerous holly trees dotted around the park.

Scene of the "Botanical Garden" at the Parque de la Isla.

Romanesque Arch located in the Parque de la Isla.

A Romantic Walk

One of the most pleasant times of year to walk down the *Paseo de la Isla* is in autumn. This is when the deciduous trees are clad in their best robes, affording the citizens out for a stroll one of the most beautiful spectacles of their urban surroundings. Moreover, the great trees are perfectly counterpointed by the works of art that have been strategically placed in the corners and recesses of the walk. Amongst the artistic features that help to recreate a Romantic atmosphere in the *Parque de la Isla* are the classical arches donated by the Count of Castilfalé, a Renaissance fountain from the Monastery of San Pedro de Arlanza, a stone cross, a baptismal font, several Romanesque capitals and above all the Romanesque portal, dating from the last third of the 12th century, taken from the Church of *Nuestra Señora de la Llana* at Cerezo de Río Tirón.

Paseo de Caballería.

*The parks of Burgos
are known all over Spain.*

ON THE OTHER SIDE OF THE RIVER

As a result of the economic and demographic evolution experienced in the second half of the 15th and the 16th centuries, the town expanded beyond the limits of its walls. The area best suited to urban development was the flat plain stretching out on the other side of the The Arlanzón. Very soon the groups of houses huddled around the main roads and the existing monasteries began to undergo considerable growth. Such is the case of the outlying district of Vega which, situated near the *Puente de Santa María,* became the focal point of Burgos 'ultra pontem' in the late Middle Ages and the early Renaissance. The neighbourhood, just as it does today, revolved around the well laid out *Plaza de Vega.*

Vega District

For many centuries this district was the point at which all travellers and merchants approaching Burgos from the south of the Peninsula prepared to enter the town. Its taverns, hostels, hospitals, churches, monasteries, workshops, shops and inns - one of which still survives from the 17th century - lent the area a great atmosphere and brought considerable prosperity. From *Plaza de la Vega,* our tour of the town runs parallel to the Arlanzón in search of further monumental landmarks. After visiting the Church of *La Merced,* we move on to the San Nicolás school. The latter was built in the 16th century in Renaissance style by Pedro de Rasines, under the patronage of Cardinal Iñigo López de Mendoza. Opposite the present-day secondary school lies the *Iglesia del Carmen,* a church built in the late 'seventies to replace the old convent established in 1611. In the interior there is a 17th-century relief of Pietá attributed to Gregorio Fernández. We continue down *Calle del Carmen* and, on crossing the railroad tracks, we come to the *Calle de Santa Dorotea.* Rising up practically at the end of this street is the convent of the nuns of the order of St Dorothy. The interior of their church holds a collection of early 16th-century sepulchres in arched recesses or arcosolia. In Gimeno district is the Renaissance Church of *San Cosme y San Damián,* the outstanding features of which are its beautiful portal by Juan de Vallejo and the remarkable baroque main altarpiece. Next we must cross the *Plaza de Vega* and take *Calle la Calera.*

A night-time view of the Monastery of Las Huelgas.

Detail of the sanctuary and the tower of the Cistercian Monastery of Las Huelgas.

Burgos Museum

In the 16th century, *Calle de la Calera* became the most grandiose road of the new area of Burgos that was evolving on the plain to the south of the river. This was where several illustrious local families established their stately homes. The most outstanding of the said families were the Miranda and the Hurtado de Mendoza. Their respective palaces, *Casa de Miranda* and *Casa de Iñigo Angulo,* still survive today and provide a noble home for the Museum of Burgos. This cultural institution is well-kept, modern and strictly didactic in appearance and as such invites visitors to make good use of all its contents. If we add to this the quality and on occasions the universal importance of the items on display, it is clear that this is one of the best museums in Spain. The visitor is first struck by the museum's magnificent central courtyard, deemed to be one of the most interesting examples of Spanish Renaissance, around which lie the *Casa de Miranda* and the museum rooms.

Cloistered Nuns

In order to round off our comprehensive tour of southern Burgos, we quickly make our way to the Santa Clara district to visit the old convent of the Franciscan order. The convent church, which we enter by means of a Gothic style portal, dates back to the second half of the 13th century and is contemporaneous with Burgos Cathedral. After admiring this austere convent, we head back towards the Arlanzón and the nearby *Plaza de Santa Teresa.* Caught up as we are in the hustle and bustle of life at the end of this millennium, it is pleasing to experience the tranquil atmosphere of recollection that hangs over the cloistered convents of the discalced Carmelites - in 1582 St Teresa of Jesus came to Burgos to carry out what would be the last of her foundations - and the Trinitarian nuns.

*Main altarpiece
of the church
at the Monastery
of Las Huelgas*

The Monastery of Las Huelgas

A stone's throw away from the town lie a series of monuments and places that are well worth an extensive visit: the Cistercian Monastery of Santa María la Real de Las Huelgas, the *Cartuja de Miraflores* (Miraflores Charterhouse) and the Monastery of *San Pedro de Cardeña,* linked to the history of El Cid.

On the outskirts of Burgos, in an area of natural meadows lined with gall and holm oaks, the Kings of Castile erected a small palace which they used for hunting and leisure purposes. Indeed, it is in the root of the word *holgar* ('to be at leisure') that the etymological origin of the name of the convent, *Las Huelgas,* is to be found. On these royal lands King Alfonso VIII was to found, on 1st June 1187, the Cistercian Monastery of Santa María la Real de las Huelgas. The foundation of a convent for Bernadine nuns had been the brainchild of Queen Eleanor, who apart from being Alfonso's wife, was the sister of the English king, Richard I 'Coeur de Lion'.

The outward appearance of the monastery reflects the interior layout habitual in Cistercian institutions under the Rule of St Bernard. Situated at El Compás de Adentro, a striking interaction of volumes is created between the long nave and aisles, the transept with its gable ends and the sturdy tower crowned with machicolations that presides the complex. According to the records, the first artist to work at Las Huelgas was master Ricardo, who in about 1203 completed the sober elevation of the church in keeping with the models of the French abbeys of Cîteaux and Fontevrault.

The chapter house at Las Huelgas is one of the marvels of Cistercian art in Spain.

The sepulchres of Alfonso VIII and Eleanor of England at the Monastery of Las Huelgas. ▶

The Royal Pantheon

After visiting the sanctuary, in order to reach the royal pantheon the visitor to the monastery church has to pass through the cloister. We are now in one of the aisles, dedicated to Santa Catalina, and the first sepulchre we see is that of the Infant Fernando de la Cerda. This is the only tomb that is still intact today and in its interior, besides the infant's mummified remains, some magnificent dresses and clothes were found that can be seen at the monastery's renowned Museum of Medieval Materials.

Resting on lions at the centre of the long, slender, translucent nave is the double sarcophagus in which Alfonso VIII and his English queen Eleanor are buried. Beneath the 13th-century image of the Descent from the Cross crowning the wall separating the cloister from the transept are the likewise interesting tombs of Doña Berenguela and Doña Blanca de Portugal, dating from the 13th and 14th centuries respectively.

Through a beautiful Gothic doorway whose wooden leaves are decorated with interesting Mudéjar tracery we come into the cloister of San Fernando. The latter is a surprising Gothic structure that combines the features of medieval Christian architecture with decorative elements from the Moslem world. Opening out on to one of the sides of this cloister is the monastery chapterhouse, regarded as the finest achievement of Cistercian architecture in Spain. The other cloister at Las Huelgas is known under the name of *Las Claustrillas* and constitutes the oldest surviving part of the monastery.

Near *Las Claustrillas* are two original architectural manifestations that alone lend the monastery complex a singular character. The first such structure is the *Capilla de la Asunción,* a true anthology of Almohad art and in its day part of the original royal palace over which Las Huelgas was built. The second is the small *Capilla de Santiago* which, situated in the monastery garden, is entered through a pointed horseshoe arch that rests on two beautiful Islamic-style capitals. The chapel interior features a spectacular Mudéjar ceiling.

*Sepulchre of John II
at the Charterhouse
of Miraflores*

*Outside view
of the
Charterhouse
of Miraflores.*

Cartuja de Miraflores

Through the shade of the leafy trees lining the *Parque de la Quinta,* right on the other side of Burgos, we come to the gently rising hill on which the Charterhouse of *Santa María de Miraflores* stands. In 1401, King Henry III the Sickly - who was born in Burgos - had a fortified palace built at Miraflores which he used on hunting expeditions. His son, John II, handed over the Miraflores palace to the Order of the Carthusians, with the intention that it be converted into a royal pantheon. Work on the Charterhouse was begun by Juan de Colonia and completed in around 1500 by Garcí Fernández de Matienzo and above all Simón de Colonia, with the firm support of Queen Isabella the Catholic.

The entire building appears impregnated with the asceticism of the Carthusians and visitors here are imbued with a pleasant feeling of peace and solitude. After admiring the slender exterior of the Charterhouse church, one must not miss its interesting interior. Featuring an aisleless nave covered by ribbed vaulting, the division of space in the church is in keeping with the habitual Carthusian practice. The sanctuary holds three masterpieces by the great artist Gil de Siloe: the main altarpiece, a true wonder of late Gothic religious imagery, the double alabaster sepulchre belonging to John II and Isabel of Portugal and the statue, under an arched recess, of the Infant Alfonso in a praying posture. Also greatly revered is the 17th-century realistic image of St Bruno by the Portuguese sculptor Manuel Pereira.

Detail of the sepulchre
of John II.

*Main altarpiece
at the Charterhouse
of Miraflores.* ▶

Detail of the relief portraying
the Last Supper on the main altarpiece
at the Charterhouse.

*Interior of the apse
at the Monastery
of San Pedro de Cardeña.*

*The Monastery of San Pedro
de Cardeña stands out against
the snow-capped peaks of the
La Demanda mountains.*

San Pedro de Cardeña

Setting out from the Charterhouse of Miraflores, once we have passed through the extensive pinewoods of the much frequented forest area called Fuentes Blancas, it is less than ten kilometres to the Monastery of *San Pedro de Cardeña*. The foundation of this old monastery is to be traced back to the early Middle Ages, to be exact the year 899. In the course of time, favoured by the first Counts of Castile, it became a centre of great religious and political influence, from which almost all the lands of the region were controlled. In the summer of 953, Cordovans under the command of Caliph Abd er-Rahman III himself, in one of their devastating expeditions, reached the gates of Cardeña and proceeded to destroy the monastery and martyrize over two hundred of its monks.

Subsequent to its reconstruction, *San Pedro was* to bear witness to the legendary feats of that Castilian hero *par excellence,* El Cid Campeador. El Cid passed through Cardeña on his way into exile, leaving his wife and two daughters here in the custody of the abbot; and on his death, he was laid to rest under the noble, sacred stones of the monastery. From the times of El Cid, all that remains are the abbey tower and the archaic Romanesque *Claustro de los Mártires.* The monastery church dates from the mid-15th century and was constructed during the abbacy of Pedro del Burgo. Apart from the Renaissance sepulchres that held the remains of El Cid and Doña Jimena - until they were transferred to Burgos in the early 19th century by the Napoleonic troops -, one can also contemplate several images of Rodrigo Díaz de Vivar, *El Cid,* on the church and monastery façades.

BURGOS WILL NOT LEAVE YOU COLD

Burgos is widely renowned for a variety of reasons, amongst which we can cite its cathedral, its lamb, its cheese, its *morcilla* or blood sausage, and its cold weather. However, it is the latter meteorological element that dominates most remarks and conversations on this Castilian city. It certainly cannot be denied that in winter, when the north wind blows, it is really cold here; nevertheless, it must also be said that each season of the year brings out the best in the town on the banks of the Arlanzón. Winter, in which a sudden snowfall may shroud the urban landscape in an evocative white blanket, is followed by a fleeting spring typical of the meseta, in which the trees are dotted with green buds and the gardens are full of the fragrance and colour of flowers. The intertwined plane trees lining the *Paseo del Espolón* awaken from their long winter's rest, covering their bare branches with a substantial canopy of large leaves that acts as a filter and a screen for the midday sun on the moderately hot summer days in the city. The cool summer nights of Burgos ease the lives of those travellers from hotter, drier parts of the country desperate for a good night's sleep. If I may offer the reader a piece of advice, I should tell him not to miss Burgos in the autumn, a season in which temperatures are fair and the town is wrapped in a thousand hues of equinoctial light.

Snowfalls embellish the streets and parks of Burgos.

Detail of the fountain in Plaza España, lit up at night.

Burgos also boasts an abundant heritage of contemporary art. ▶

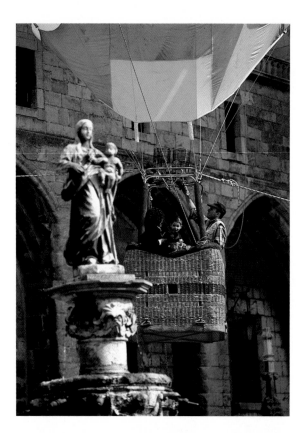

▲ The «Gigantillos» are the main atracttion. ▶
Balloon in Plaza Santa María.
　　One of the handicraft workshops in Burgos.

Should one have no time or simply not wish to have a large meal, it is a good idea to visit one of the excellent bars and mesones that abound in Burgos and have some tapas or order a small serving of a variety of items such as patatas bravas *(sauteed potatoes in a spicy sauce);* cojonudos *(quail's eggs with smoked susage);* capataces; gambas rebozadas *(prawns in batter);* calamares *(fried squid);* tigres *(mussels);* caracoles *(snails);* pinchos de bonito *(tuna with bread);* gildas; huevos rellenos *(stuffed eggs); and* bacalao y anchoas rebozadas *(cod and anchovies in batter).*

Sopa castellana.

Picadillo. The wholesome cuisine of Burgos is one of tastiest in Spain.

*The River Arlanzón
flowing under
San Pablo bridge.*

Eating in Burgos

After having steeped one's mind in the history, art and culture that Burgos exudes on all corners, there is nothing better than a good meal to refresh one's tired body. The cuisine on offer in Burgos will not disappoint even the most demanding of gourmets. The indecisive among us may find it impossible to choose when faced with such a long list of equally tasty specialities, but I shall nevertheless suggest the following: *sopa castellana* and *sopa burgalesa; olla podrida* (pulse stew); *lentejas medievales* (lentil dish); *morcilla de Burgos* (locally made blood sausage); *picadillo* (spicy mince dish); *ensalada de berros* (watercress salad); *escabechados* (marinated fish); *cecina* (cured pork); *mollejas de cordero* (lamb sweetbread); *manitas de cordero o cerdo* (lamb's feet or pig's trotters); *asadurilla* (offal); *codornices estofadas* (braised quails); *perdiz a la cazadora* (partridge dish); *liebre con setas* (hare with mushrooms); j*abalí con patatas* (wild boar with potatoes); *corzo de la Demanda* (La Demanda venison); *asado de cordero lechal* (roast suckling lamb); *chuletillas de cordero a la brasa* (grilled lamb chops); and for dessert, besides the famous *queso fresco* or soft Burgos cheese, one can try *el postre del abuelo; torrijas con miel de Cascajares* (bread soaked in milk and egg and fried in Cascajares honey); *natillas* (custard); *cerezas* or cherries from Covarrubias and Oña; *cuajada natural* (curd) and *yemas de canónigo* (sugared egg yolks). A golden rule when dining or having snacks in Burgos is to accompany the food with a good *Ribera del Duero* red wine.

A charming detail of the Calle Vitoria in Burgos.

Sunset seen from the Castle Park. ▶

Burgos is a town full of walks.

A narrow street of the medieval town.

Statue in the Plaza del Espolón.

Typical glassed balconies in Burgos.

A wide variety of fairs and markets are held in Burgos.

The standard of Las Navas in the Curpillos procession. ▶

Festivities and Celebrations

The most original and deep-rooted of the festivities in Burgos is that of the *Fiesta del Curpillos,* which is celebrated each year on the Friday after Corpus Christi (although recently it has been held a few days later) near the Monastery of *Las Huelgas.* One of the most popular and traditional events still surviving in Burgos, this is the moment when the *Pendón* or standard from the battle of Navas de Tolosa is displayed to the citizens. Borne by the highest-ranking military official, this spectacular trophy of war is accompanied on its way through the Las Huelgas district by a solemn procession including the canopied Holy Sacrament, the town authorities, local groups of dancers and the *gigantes y gigantillos* (huge carnival figures). Once the official ceremony is over, the people of Burgos meet in the nearby park, *El Parral,* where a popular picnic is held. Blood sausage, spicy mince and pig's snout *(morro)* are some of the gastronomic delights that are savoured in the cool shade of the century-old poplars. Also worthy of mention are the feast days of St Peter and St Paul and the religious celebrations in commemoration of St Adelelmus the Abbot.

SILOS
AND COVARRUBIAS

The Arlanza, Castile's mythological river *par excellence,* in whose waters the legendary faces of the kingdom's founder heroes were once reflected, constitutes the backbone of an area whose outstanding geographical features are the spectacular rocky cliffs of *Las Mamblas,* mounts Valdosa and Gayúbar, the craggy terrain of Cervera, the Carazo meseta and the canyon of Mataviejas and La Yecla. Sheltering amidst this veritable labyrinth of superb landscape, lined with the most important juniper groves in the world, is an abundant and varied population of birds of prey. In addition to all this natural beauty, just a few kilometres away lie two world-renowned architectural wonders, namely the Monastery of Santo Domingo de Silos and the medieval town of Covarrubias.

Aerial view of the monastery and village of Santo Domingo de Silos.

Next pages:
Passeway of the Romanesque cloister at Silos.
Detail of the cloister and the famous cypress at Silos.

Santo Domingo de Silos

In the southeastern section of Burgos province, in a steep, hidden valley cut by the River Mataviejas between the enormous bare crags of Cervera and the legendary heights of the Carazo meseta, we come across Santo Domingo de Silos.

Before entering the village itself, the elegant silhouette of a haughty cypress tree tells us that we are approaching one of the marvels of western Christian art, namely the Romanesque cloister of the Monastery of Santo Domingo de Silos. A careful study of the cloister enables us to refute the first impression that many visitors have on coming into the heart of the monastery. It is not a perfect square. The ground plan of the cloister is in fact an irregular quadrilateral whose sides do not stand at right angles to each other. The southern and northern galleries are longer and comprise 16 arches, whereas those facing east and west are slightly smaller and have only 14 arches each.

Relief portraying the "Doubt of St Thomas".

The cober of the tomb of St Dominic.

Detail of the apothecary laboratory at Silos.

Another singular, outstanding feature of the cloister at Silos is its two superimposed storeys. The magnificent final effect produced by the cloister would lead one to believe that the harmony, the sense of proportion and the mathematic regularity expressed in the combination of reliefs, columns, capitals and arches were part of a preconceived plan that was hardly altered in the course of the hundred years that its construction lasted. The controversy surrounding this enigmatic Romanesque structure does not only concern its chronology - the late 11th and most of the 12th centuries -, but also the number of masters that worked throughout the said period of time in order to create what is one of the wonders of medieval European art. The main feature that makes the cloister of the Monastery of Santo Domingo de Silos unique in European Romanesque architecture is the originality of most of the motifs sculpted on the reliefs - eight magnificent portrayals of scenes from the life of Christ - and on the capitals of this veritable museum of sculpture. The iconographical sources that inspired the various artists that worked on the cloister can be traced both to the decorations of the Persian and Islamic cloths and ivories that were imported from the east and to the miniature manuscripts - almost all Mozarabic - that were being copied in the late 11th century at the monastery scriptorium.

Other aspects of *Santo Domingo de Silos* worth seeing are the original coffering in the cloister ceiling, one of the best preserved apothecaries in Spain, the museum with its collection of medieval enamelled objects, the interesting library and the church - in which one can still hear Gregorian chant performed by Benedictine monks - built by Ventura Rodríguez to replace the original Romanesque structure.

Doña Urraca Tower at Covarrubias.

The Collegiate of San Cosme y San Damián. ▶

The Town of Covarrubias

The singular medieval profile of Covarrubias rises up against the suggestive, sheer limestone reliefs of the Las Mamblas mountains and the winding course of the River Arlanza. Dominated by the outlines of the sturdy fortified tower of Doña Urraca and the Gothic collegiate church of *San Cosme y San Damián,* this famous town evokes its splendrous past at every turn. The visitor should roam its well laid out cobbled streets and squares and enjoy its original popular architecture, which includes a large number of timber-framed houses featuring large juniper beams, the most noteworthy of which is the medieval house of Doña Sancha.

The traveller is also pleasantly surprised by the artistic heritage awaiting him in this breezy town. Considered the most interesting of all its monuments are the tower of Doña Urraca or Fernán González and the collegiate church. The former was erected at the beginning of the 10th century over earlier remains and is without doubt the oldest, best-preserved example of medieval fortified architecture in Burgos. Shaped like a truncated pyramid and featuring a rectangular base, the tower stands an impressive 22 metres tall and is crowned by ten machicolations added in the 15th century.

The collegiate church of *San Cosme y San Damián* is an elegant Gothic structure with a nave and two aisles, built over a previous church which legend attributes to the Visigothic King Chindasuinth. Buried

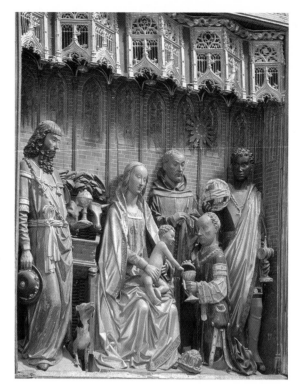

Detail of the Covarrubias triptych.

Popular architecture at Covarrubias.

inside the church are the remains of Fernán González, the first independent Count of Castile, and those of his wife, Doña Sancha, who herself rests in a beautiful Hispano-Roman sarcophagus. Other treasures of the church are its famous 17th-century organ, the cloister where the Norwegian princess Christina was laid to rest, and the parish museum featuring a magnificent 15th-century triptych portraying the Adoration of the Magi.

The Gothic Church of *Santo Tomás,* the arch by Juan de Herrera commemorating the Adelantamiento or frontier status of Castile, the Town Hall, the refurbished tavern, a stone column marking the limits of Covarrubias and a pair of stone crosses complete the rich heritage of a town that the visitor must not leave without having tasted some of the local gastronomic delights, such as the pulse stew, roast suckling lamb and kid goat, and cherries. All washed down with a good Ribera de Arlanza wine.